By William O. Douglas

OF MEN AND MOUNTAINS

STRANGE LANDS AND FRIENDLY PEOPLE

BEYOND THE HIGH HIMALAYAS

NORTH FROM MALAYA

AN ALMANAC OF LIBERTY

WE THE JUDGES

RUSSIAN JOURNEY

THE RIGHT OF THE PEOPLE

EXPLORING THE HIMALAYAS

WEST OF THE INDUS

AMERICA CHALLENGED

DEMOCRACY'S MANIFESTO

MY WILDERNESS: THE PACIFIC WEST

A LIVING BILL OF RIGHTS

MY WILDERNESS: EAST TO KATAHDIN

THE ANATOMY OF LIBERTY

FREEDOM OF THE MIND

MR. LINCOLN AND THE NEGROES

A WILDERNESS BILL OF RIGHTS

THE BIBLE AND THE SCHOOLS

The Bible
and the Schools

The Bible
and the Schools

by WILLIAM O. DOUGLAS

LITTLE, BROWN AND COMPANY, BOSTON, TORONTO

Published simultaneously in Canada
by Little, Brown & Company (Canada) Limited

PRINTED IN THE UNITED STATES OF AMERICA

FIRST AMENDMENT

"Congress shall make no law respecting an establishment of religion, or prohibiting the free exercise thereof . . ."

This brochure has its roots in a lecture that was scheduled to be delivered before the Phi Beta Kappa Associates in New York City on November 22, 1963 — a dark and sad day in American history. The assassination of the late President caused the cancellation of that lecture and its deferment for a year, during which time the paper I had prepared grew to its present proportions. I am deeply indebted to Joan M. Douglas and Dagmar Hamilton for their help in giving the original lecture new dimensions.

WILLIAM O. DOUGLAS

Foreword

... THE Supreme Court has made its judgment and a good many people obviously will disagree with it. Others will agree with it. But I think that it is important for us if we are going to maintain our constitutional principle that we support the Supreme Court decisions even when we may not agree with them.

In addition, we have in this case a very easy remedy and that is to pray ourselves. And I would think that it would be a welcome reminder to every American family that we can pray a good deal more at home, we can attend our churches with a good deal more fidelity, and we can make the true meaning of prayer much more important in the lives of all of our children. That power is very much open to us. And I would hope that as a result of this decision that all American parents will intensify their efforts at home, and the rest of us will support the Constitution and the responsibility of the Supreme Court in interpreting it, which is theirs, and given to them by the Constitution.

Public Papers of the Presidents, John F. Kennedy, 1962, pp. 510–511.

The Bible
and the Schools

I

WE Americans are a religious people and prayer plays an important role in our lives. We have instinctively turned to God in prayer for protection from disaster, for deliverance from evil, or for the achievement of some other goal. A prayer is a reaching out on the part of the human mind to a power beyond itself. Being a predominantly Christian people, we have in our prayers followed the example of Jesus Christ.

We are truthfully one nation "under God" and our institutions "presuppose a Divine Being" (*Zorach* v. *Clauson,* 343 U.S. 306, 313). Those propositions are not a matter of speculation, for the First Amendment bars the federal government from enacting any law *"respecting an establishment of religion, or prohibiting the free exercise thereof."*

The Fourteenth Amendment provides that *no state shall "deprive any person of . . . liberty . . . without due process of law."* The word "liberty" in that clause has been held to mean the liberties guaranteed by the First Amendment (*Schneider* v. *State,* 308 U.S.

147, 160; *Cantwell* v. *Connecticut,* 310 U.S. 296, 303).

Thus the Constitution has been construed to mean that neither the federal government nor the States can pass a law "respecting an establishment of religion, or prohibiting the free exercise thereof."

It is the concern of the Free Exercise Clause that every person worship as he please or not worship at all. Perhaps he is an atheist or agnostic and if he were able to summon enough votes he could put legal barriers in the way of the "free exercise" of others. No atheist or agnostic, however — or any combination of them — has that power. Nor may those who believe in one faith use their power to make nonconformists worship as they do. Thus the First and the Fourteenth Amendments, by making religious liberty available to all, without discrimination, implicitly recognize that men have a relation to God that is in their own keeping and free from interference by others. This is tacit recognition that our regime is "under God" and not under the command of nonbelievers. There would be no place for the Free Exercise Clause of the First Amendment in an atheistic society. As the United States Supreme Court stated in *Abington School District* v. *Schempp,* (374 U.S. 213), many of our institutional practices, including our oaths of office, honor the Supreme Being whom our religion teaches us to worship. Moreover, we are Christian because the vast majority of our people profess a Western religion, not one of the East. But that is not the reason why it would violate the Establishment Clause to require Moslem prayers in public schools. Eastern religions, whether Hindu, Buddhist, or Islam, are as much protected by the First Amendment as any other. They are indeed not any more esoteric than the one which *United States* v. *Ballard* (322 U.S. 78) protected. There the religious sect was the I AM movement, whose leaders claimed the power to communicate with Jesus, George Washington, and others, to transmit messages to the living, and to heal persons of ailments and diseases. They were charged in a criminal prosecution with using the mails to defraud in promoting their religious creed. The narrow issue was whether the trial court was warranted in submitting to the jury these people's bona fide belief in this creed. The Supreme Court held that the truth or verity of these doctrines or beliefs were not triable issues.

A person cannot be put to the proof of his religious doctrines or beliefs. If he could, then heresy trials and powerful divisive forces could be reintroduced into our society. If they could, then men could be sent to jail because they practiced or taught a religion in which the jury did not believe. Truth of the religious belief — like sincerity in embracing it — is foreclosed even where the practitioners are charged with a fraudulent intrigue. Religious experience is beyond the competence of courts and juries to prove or disprove.

[5]

The "free exercise" of religion has not been taken literally so as to include any practice a "believer" embraces. While religious belief may not be tested or challenged in court, religious practice may be. There have been in the world's history many extreme measures that have passed muster under religious practice. Human sacrifice is one. The temples of Venus along the Phoenician coast were once the sites of promiscuous sexual intercourse. The question was raised under the Free Exercise Clause as to the propriety of polygamy. Under Mormon doctrine, prior to its reformation, failure to practice polygamy, circumstances permitting, would result in "damnation in the life to come." When Utah was a territory, Congress legislated against polygamy there, making it a crime. A devout Mormon who practiced polygamy was convicted and his conviction was sustained in *Reynolds* v. *United States* (98 U.S. 145) against the claim that the statute violated the Free Exercise Clause of the First Amendment. In those prosecutions for bigamy and in other ways such as denial of voting rights (*Murphy* v. *Ramsey,* 114 U.S. 15; *Davis* v. *Beason,* 133 U.S. 333) the legislature was sustained in placing sanctions in favor of monogamy and against polygamy. The Court indeed went so far in *Mormon Church* v. *United States* (136 U.S. 1) as to sustain an Act of Congress that confiscated all property of the Mormon Church (except houses of worship, parsonages, and burial grounds) and authorized their

[6]

sale, the proceeds to be applied to the benefit of common schools in the Utah Territory. That action was taken because the Mormon Church at that time practiced and preached polygamy, a practice that the Court termed "barbarous" and "contrary to the spirit of Christianity and of the civilization which Christianity has produced in the western world" (*Ibid.*, p. 49). And the power of Congress to dissolve that religious organization was based on the fact that it was organized under the laws of the Territory of Utah, over which Congress had jurisdiction, including power to alter corporate charters.

Thus acts deemed by the people inimical to the peace, good order, and morals of a free society can be banned, notwithstanding the First Amendment.

One religious sect — Jehovah's Witnesses — believed and taught that saluting a flag was bowing down to a "graven image" contrary to the Biblical command. A state required the flag salute from all children on penalty of expulsion from school. Children of Jehovah's Witnesses refused to perform the ceremony, because in their view it would be bowing down to a "graven image" contrary to the teachings of Exodus 20:4, 5. School officials retaliated by expelling these children from school, by threatening to send them to reformatories for criminally inclined juveniles, and by prosecuting the parents for causing delinquency. Suit was brought in *West Virginia Board* v. *Barnette* (319 U.S. 624) for an injunction against the operation

[7]

of the law on the ground that it violated the Free Exercise Clause. The Court held the requirement to be unconstitutional, saying, "If there is any fixed star in our constitutional constellation, it is that no official, high or petty, can prescribe what shall be orthodox in politics, nationlism, religion, or other matters or opinion or force citizens to confess by word or act their faith therein" (*Ibid.*, p. 642, and see *Taylor* v. *Mississippi,* 319 U.S. 583).

Religious groups take up collections, sell religious literature, and engage in other fund-raising activities. The matter was put humorously by the comedian Bob Hope: "Once I was flying in a plane that was hit by lightning. 'Do something religious,' a little old lady across the aisle suggested. So I did — I took up a collection." Fund-raising for churches is, of course, essential to the free exercise of religion, for many aspects of worshiping entail expenditures of funds. Some communities license solicitors of funds. But churchmen or others on church fund-raising projects cannot constitutionally be required to obtain a license. The point is illustrated in cases like *Murdock* v. *Pennsylvania* (319 U.S. 105, where a municipality sought to bar Jehovah's Witnesses from distributing their religious literature, i.e., selling it at a price, without a license, and by *Jameson* v. *Texas* [318 U.S. 413], where a city barred the distribution of handbills along the streets. The exaction in the first case and the prohibition in the second were held invalid by

[8]

the Court, the distribution of religious literature being in the tradition of the ancient colporteur who went among the people handing out religious literature and asking alms.

The Free Exercise Clause is two-edged. It allows anyone to worship as he chooses, to embrace such creed or dogma as suits him, to affiliate himself with the religious group of his choice. By the same token it allows a person to reject all faiths and to embrace atheism or agnosticism. The Free Exercise Clause is reinforced by Article VI of the Constitution, which in part provides that ". . . no religious test shall ever be required as a qualification to any office or public trust under the United States." In *Torcaso* v. *Watkins* (367 U.S. 488), a man was refused a commission as notary public because he would not declare his belief in God. Maryland required occupants of all state offices to make that declaration. It was held to be an unconstitutional requirement because of the Free Exercise Clause and Article VI. "This Maryland religious test for public office unconstitutionally invades the appellant's freedom of belief and religion and therefore cannot be enforced against him" (*Ibid.*, p. 496).

As we shall see, that harks back to "establishment" practices of the states prior to 1789.

During the last century, when Protestants dominated the electorate, many public schools introduced sectarian education by Bible-reading and otherwise. The Roman Catholics rebelled, as will be noted. One product of the rebellion was the increased tempo for establishment of parochial schools, the constitutionality of which did not reach the Court until 1925. The case came from Oregon, where a state statute required all children between eight and sixteen to attend public schools so long as they had not completed the eighth grade. Enforcement of that law was sought to be enjoined. The Court held for the parochial school, thus giving religious liberty of parents and children a new reach. The idea of religious liberty written into the First and Fourteenth Amendments was said to exclude any general power of the states "to standardize its children by forcing them to accept instruction from public teachers only" (*Pierce* v. *Society of Sisters*, 268 U.S. 510,535).

The Free Exercise Clause thus protects the individual from any coercive measure that encourages him toward one faith or creed, discourages him from another, or makes it prudent or desirable for him to select one and embrace it. As the Supreme Court of South Dakota held in *State* v. *Weedman* (55 So. Dak. 343), expulsion of Roman Catholic students from public schools because of their refusal to attend readings of the King James Bible was a violation of their right of free exercise of religion. So far as government is concerned, a person can be a believer or nonbeliever, a churchman or an atheist, a proselytizer or a hermit — as he chooses.

Occasionally the Free Exercise Clause and the

Establishment Clause overlap. If government introduces religious education into public schools, it violates the Establishment Clause (see *McCollum* v. *Board of Education,* 333 U.S. 203) as it puts the weight of the school system behind a particular creed, dogma, or faith. Borderline cases have arisen. Suppose a public school system provides for a break in the daily school work so that students can attend religious services off the school property. Public schools make that kind of accommodation by recessing for Saturdays and Sundays. Can they make other like accommodations during the school week? The Court held it permissible in *Zorach* v. *Clauson,* (343 U.S. 306), provided, however, that if coercion is used to get students to use the public school recess to attend religious services then there is a violation of the Free Exercise Clause.

It may be that religious exercise in a public school has inherent in it the element of compulsion on the nonconformist child. Seymour Graubard stated, while testifying on behalf of the Anti-Defamation League of B'nai B'rith, on the proposed Becker Amendment,[1] to which I will refer:

I was brought up in New York City. I went to a public school which had possibly 40 percent Jewish children. We had delightful times at Christmas. It was a gay holiday. We had no sense of restriction because

[1] School Prayers, Hearings, House Committee on the Judiciary, 88th Cong. 2nd Sess. Serial No. 9, Pt. II, p. 1240.

[11]

there were no religious ceremonies as such in this holiday. The teachers understood the nature of the class, partly Protestant, partly Catholic, and partly Jewish, and took pains to see to it that there were no observances which could cause embarrassment to any of the children. I have a very warm regard for those religious recollections of holidays of tradition.

They extended to Easter, as well, in my public school.

On the other hand, my wife who went to public school in Rutland, Vt., has told me of how in her elementary schools she was one of two Jewish children in her class, of how it was generally the case that Christmas would be a time of religious ceremony in the class. She felt out of sorts, out of place, and felt separated from the rest of her students by the need that she felt of not participating in an out-and-out religious ceremony.

But that kind of issue has never been finally resolved in the courts.

Sunday Blue Laws have been enforced even as against members of religious sects whose Sabbath is Saturday, not Sunday (*Braunfeld* v. *Brown*, 366 U.S. 599). The result is that those whose Sabbath is not Sunday can be forced under threat of criminal penalties to observe two Sabbaths. It was held, however, that while these laws in their far-distant origin served a religious end, they can be sustained in their modern setting as health measures (*McGowan* v. *Maryland*, 366 U.S. 420). But in *Sherbert* v. *Verner* (374 U.S. 398), a state law was struck down which disqualified a Seventh-day Adventist for unemployment compensation benefits solely because of her refusal to accept employment in which she would have to work on Saturday, contrary to her religious belief. A state may not thus penalize a person because of his or her religious convictions any more than it may exclude a person from receiving the benefits of public welfare legislation because of his or her religious faith or lack of it (*Ibid.*, p. 410).

Moreover, there may at times be a seeming clash between the Establishment Clause and the Free Exercise Clause. The use of public funds to build chapels and provide chaplains at military establishments for members of the armed services is one instance; and the furnishing of like facilities in state and federal penal institutions is another. Yet the people involved — members of the armed services and prisoners — have been deprived of their usual opportunity to worship as they choose. Therefore it is said that government may provide the facilities lest those groups be deprived of their free exercise rights. No coercion is involved; merely a gap is being filled which otherwise would lead to a denial of a constitutional right.

The Free Exercise Clause bars the state from running church affairs. For example, the New York legislature undertook in 1945 to deprive the prelate of the Russian Orthodox Church, who had been appointed by the Moscow ecclesiastical authorities, of possession of the New York cathedral and to grant possession to a patriarch chosen by an American separatist group. Though property rights were involved, the conflict was generated by a clash of religious faiths. In that event the civil courts are open for adjudication of the dispute. But they decide the controversy on the basis of the ecclesiastical law of the particular church (*Watson* v. *Jones,* 13 Wall. 379). If that were not true then the state would be a referee applying *secular* standards for the resolution of internal ecclesiastical or theological controversies. This would put the civil authorities astride religious institutions as respects some of their innermost concerns (see *Gonzalez* v. *Archbishop,* 280 U.S. 1, 16–17).

With that background the Court held that New York had no authority to intervene in the religious conflict that raged within the Russian Orthodox Church (*Kedroff* v. *St. Nicholas Cathedral,* 344 U.S. 94). The court, after examining the ecclesiastical law, concluded that under it the New York cathedral was subject to the dominion of the Moscow Archbishop. To let state legislation regulate Church affairs, the Court said, would be to interfere with "the free exercise of religion" (*Ibid.,* p. 107). The purpose of the New York legislation was to protect the American churches from Communist infiltration. The Court's answer was simple:

"Legislative power to punish subversive action cannot be doubted. If such action should be actually attempted by a cleric, neither his robe nor his pulpit would be a defense. But in this case no problem of punishment for the violation of law arises. There is no charge of subversive or hostile action by any ecclesiastic. Here there is a transfer by statute of control over churches. This violates our rule of separation between church and state" (*Ibid.*, pp. 109–110). A state legislature is not free, the Court concluded, to resolve religious disputes over property by applying secular standards: ". . . When the property right follows as an incident from decisions of the church custom or law on ecclesiastical issues, the church rule controls. This under our Constitution necessarily follows in order that there may be free exercise of religion" (*Ibid.*, pp. 120–121). The Mormon case, *Latter-Day Saints* v. *United States* (136 U.S. 1), already noted, where a church was dissolved, was distinguished because of the presence in that case of the unlawful practice of polygamy.

There are, of course, many permissible accommodations between Church and State without violating either the Free Exercise Clause or the Establishment Clause. Police — who are, of course, municipal or state employees — direct traffic at churches or help parishioners across the street. Fire departments answer the alarm when the church is on fire. Veterans get government grants to complete their education and many spend that government money in parochial schools (72 Stat. 1175). Inexpensive school lunches are available under an Act of Congress (60 Stat. 233) for both public and private school children. Private and parochial schools, as well as public schools, are reimbursed for the education of pages who work in Congress and at the Supreme Court. (60 Stat. 839). Churches are usually granted exemption from taxation. It was accordingly held in *Everson* v. *Board of Education* (330 U.S. 1, 17) that taxpayers' money could constitutionally be used to pay "the bus fares of parochial school pupils as a part of the general program under which" the fares of pupils attending public and other schools were paid.

Many have thought that one way of "establishing" a religion would be to finance it. Some indeed have concluded that that would be the very best way of "establishing" a particular religion just as it would be for establishing a foundation or any other institution. The Court said by way of *dictum* in the *Everson* case: "No tax in any amount, large or small, can be levied to support any religious activities or institutions, whatever they may be called, or whatever form they may adopt to teach or practice religion" (*Ibid.*, p. 16). The allowance of fringe benefits to students of parochial schools, however, was thought by a majority of the Court to be in quite a different tradition.

It was in this setting that the "prayer cases" were decided.

II

THE "prayer cases" arose as follows:

In New York a school board, acting on the recommendation of the Board of Regents, directed the school principal to cause the following prayer to be said aloud by each class in the presence of a teacher at the beginning of each school day:

"Almighty God, we acknowledge our dependence upon Thee, and we beg Thy blessings upon us, our parents, our teachers and our Country."

The parents of ten pupils challenged the prayer requirement, saying the official prayer was contrary to the beliefs, religions, or religious practices of themselves and their children. They were Jews, Unitarians, Ethical Culturists, and nonbelievers. This suit ended in *Engel* v. *Vitale* (370 U.S. 421), in which the Court held that the official prayer violated the Establishment Clause.

Next came *Abington School District* v. *Schempp* and *Murray* v. *Curlett* (374 U.S. 203). Those cases involved laws of Pennsylvania and Maryland, and the protesting parents and children were Unitarians

[17]

and atheists. These states required readings from the
Bible and recitations of the Lord's Prayer. In the
Maryland case the King James Version of the Bible
was used; in the Pennsylvania case the King James,
the Douay, the Revised Standard, and the Jewish
versions were each used from time to time. The
Court held the official readings violated the Establishment Clause. Some have said that the Court
should have based the decision on the Free Exercise Clause and that if it had the decisions would
have been correct. But no element of coercion was
in the cases. Students could absent themselves or,
if they remained, they were not required to participate
in the service. And there was no showing in the
record that, in spite of those safeguards, the prayer
or Bible-reading ceremonies had a coercive effect on
the children of objecting parents.

III

Every one of our colonies had to a degree some union between Church and State. Some were more tolerant of religious minorities than were others. The colony of Plymouth was ruled by a governor and a small and highly select theological aristocracy, a church-state with various grades of citizenship and noncitizenship. Puritan persecuted Quaker, as before him Roman Catholic had persecuted Protestant and Anglican persecuted Puritan.

Anne Hutchinson and Roger Williams were banished from Massachusetts and William Robinson, Marmaduke Stevenson, Mary Dyer and William Laddra were hanged for expressing views which clashed with the then prevailing "establishment." The Salem witch hunts of 1691 are, of course, notorious. Maryland became the home of religious toleration under the Catholic Calvert, extending free exercise of religion to all Christian sects except the Unitarians and to all others except the Jews. It was not long, however, before religious control changed and Roman Catholics and Episcopalians were banned. For part of the seventeenth century, Jews, Quakers, and Lutherans were persecuted in New York. The account is fully stated for each colony in the books listed in the Appendix, especially in Marnell's *The First Amendment*. But by the time of the American Revolution, experience had taught the new states that an accommodation of conflicting religious enterprises was essential; and that the best way to assure individual liberty and fair treatment to each sect was to separate Church and State.

Roger Williams, who left Massachusetts to found Rhode Island — one of the most tolerant of the early colonies — wrote eloquently in 1655:

There goes many a ship to sea, with many hundreds of souls in one ship, whose weal and woe is common, and is a true picture of a commonwealth or a human combination or society. It hath fallen out sometimes that both Papists and Protestants, Jews and Turks, may be embarked in one ship; upon which supposal I affirm that all the liberty of conscience that ever I pleaded for turns upon these two hinges — that none of the Papists, Protestants, Jews, or Turks be forced to come to the ship's prayers or worship, nor compelled from their own particular prayers or worship, if they practice any. I further add that I never denied that, notwithstanding this liberty, the commander of this ship ought to command the ship's course, yea, and also command that justice, peace, and sobriety be kept and practiced both among the seamen and all the passengers.[1]

[1] Wright, L. B., *The Cultural Life of the American Colonies, 1607–1763* (1957), p. 85.

Many have doubted if we of the twentieth century have reached so advanced a position as the one held by Roger Williams in the seventeenth century.[2]

In spite of regimes of intolerance, free exercise of religion was less of a problem in the colonies than "establishment," although the two were closely connected in history. Thus when only those of a particular faith or creed could hold office or exercise political rights, free exercise was impaired, as it was when dissenters were required to attend services of the dominant faith. When only certain ministers could perform marriages and conduct burial services, some religions got preferences and the free exercise of other religions was discouraged. Thus the struggle for disestablishment of one church or multiple churches was part and parcel of the struggle for free exercise of religion. That is as true today as it was in the eighteenth century, for the requirement of a catechism in a public school exercise will take its toll of dissenters, now as then.

Establishment took various forms: penalties or disabilities on dissenters; preferences to one or more churches either as respects economic emoluments of its officials or political rights of its members; submission of dissenters to a dominant creed; and the payment of tax to support churches. It was the use of public

[2] Marnell, William Henry, *The First Amendment* (1964), p. 102; Beth, Loren P., *The American Theory of Church and State* (1958), pp. 53-55.

funds to finance the churches and their activities that moved Madison to action.

In 1785 a bill in the Virginia legislature proposed a tax for the support of teachers of the Christian religion. That was the occasion for Madison's Memorial and Remonstrance Against Religious Assessment in which he stated:

The Religion then of every man must be left to the conviction and conscience of every man; and it is the right of every man to exercise it as these may dictate. This right is in its nature an unalienable right. It is unalienable; because the opinions of men, depending only on the evidence contemplated by their own minds, cannot follow the dictates of other men: It is unalienable also; because what is here a right towards men, is a duty towards the Creator. It is the duty of every man to render to the Creator such homage, and such only, as he believes to be acceptable to him. This duty is precedent both in order of time and degree of obligation, to the claims of Civil Society. Before any man can be considered as a member of Civil Society, he must be considered as a subject of the Governor of the Universe: And if a member of Civil Society, who enters into any subordinate Association, must always do it with a reservation of his duty to the general authority; much more must every man who becomes a member of any particular Civil Society, do it with a saving of his allegiance to the Universal Sovereign. We maintain therefore that in matters of Religion, no man's right is abridged by the Institution of Civil Society, and that Religion is wholly exempt from its cognizance. True it is, that no other rule exists, by which any question which may divide a Society, can be ultimately determined, but the will of the majority; but it is also true, that the majority may trespass on the rights of the minority.[3]

Madison's specific target was a tax collected to pay teachers of Christianity. Tax-paid teachers, who lead only in prayer, are but modified versions of Madison's target.

In his Memorial and Remonstrance, Madison referred to the history of the sectarian state.

". . . experience witnesseth that ecclesiastical establishments, instead of maintaining the purity and efficacy of Religion, have had a contrary operation. During almost fifteen centuries, has the legal establishment of Christianity been on trial. What have been its fruits? More or less in all places, pride and indolence in the Clergy; ignorance and servility in the laity; in both, superstition, bigotry and persecution."[4]

It would seem to those fresh from some Islam-dominated nations or from parts of Latin America that he was speaking in modern terms, where the clergy and the *status quo* are wedded and work together to make sure that if the common man receives any decencies of life, it will be in the Hereafter, not during his brief sojourn on earth.

There were few religious groups that did not covet

[3] Madison, James, *The Writings of James Madison* (Hunt ed. 1901), II, 183 *et seq.*
[4] *Ibid.*, II, 187, n. 3.

being beneficiaries of an "established" religion. In a letter to Monroe on April 12, 1785, Madison castigated the Presbyterians for criticizing the established church yet wanting to be included:

". . . the Presbyterians . . . seem as ready to set up an establishment which is to take them in as they were to pull down that which shut them out. I do not know a more shameful contrast than might be found between their memorials on the latter & former occasion."[5]

Freedom of religion, Madison told the Virginia convention in 1788, ". . . arises from that multiplicity of sects, which pervades America, and which is the best and only security for religious liberty in any society. For where there is such a variety of sects, there cannot be a majority of any one sect to oppress and persecute the rest."[6]

Jefferson, in his Notes on Virginia, stated the same view: "Difference of opinion is advantageous in religion. The several sects perform the office of a *censor morum* over each other. Is uniformity attainable? Millions of innocent men, women, and children, since the introduction of Christianity, have been burnt, tortured, fined, imprisoned; yet we have not advanced one inch toward uniformity."[7]

Jefferson took the position that "The way to silence

[5] *Ibid.*, I, 132, n. 3.
[6] *Ibid.*, V, 176, n. 3.
[7] *The Writings of Jefferson* (Memorial ed., 1903), II, 223.

47000

religious disputes is to take no notice of them."[8] A biographer of Jefferson has said:

"Furthermore, he noted that the dissenters now outnumbered the Anglicans. He had seen plenty of them in Albemarle, and they were specially strong in the Piedmont country generally. He did not assert that they were persecuted. On the contrary, he observed that after a century of dominance, the spirit of the Anglicans had subsided into moderation. The laws remained oppressive, however, and the spirit of the dissenters 'had risen to a degree of determination which commanded respect.' "[9]

An establishment of religion can be achieved in several ways. "The church and state can be one; the church may control the state or the state may control the church; or the relationship may take one of several possible forms of a working arrangement between the two bodies. Under all of these arrangements the church typically has a place in the state's budget, and church law usually governs such matters as baptism, marriage, divorce and separation, at least for its members and sometimes for the entire body politic" (*Abington School District* v. *Schempp*, 374 U.S. 213, 227).

An "establishment" of religion did not always mean a complete or total monopoly granted one religious

[8] *Ibid.*, p. 224.
[9] Malone, Dumas, *Jefferson the Virginian* (1948), I, 276–277.

group by government. The idea of "establishment" also meant preferences to one group. Thus, in Virginia, part and parcel of "establishment" was a preference given the Episcopalians. Before 1780, only Episcopal clergymen could perform marriages, for which a fee was charged.[10] From 1780 to 1784, "Episcopal clergymen could perform marriage ceremonies anywhere, but ministers of the other denominations could do so only in the county where they lived."[11]

In Massachusetts, only members of the Congregationalist Church had the right to vote.[12]

In the late seventeenth century the Church of England was established as the church in Maryland and the church tax set at forty pounds of tobacco per "poll." Maryland, to discourage Roman Catholic immigrants from settling there, passed laws forbidding them to have arms (even though this was then a wilderness area) and placed a tax of twenty pounds on the head of each Irishman entering the colony as a servant.[13] In most colonies, the preferred church was given land, known as glebe; its ministers were paid by the state; its churches were kept in repair;

10 Stokes, Anson Phelps, *Church and State in the United States* (1950), p. 383.

11 Beveridge, Albert J., *The Life of John Marshall* (1916), p. 221.

12 Antieau, Chester J., *Freedom from Federal Establishment: The Formation and Early History of the First Amendment Religion Clauses* (1964), p. 13.

13 *Ibid.*, p. 18.

and it occasionally received the exclusive right to hold a public lottery — a form of direct grant.[14]

Prior to 1787 there were religious qualifications for a seat in the legislature. As Cobb says: ". . . in only two out of the thirteen [states] was full and perfect freedom conceded by law. These were Rhode Island and Virginia. Six of the states, viz. New Hampshire, Connecticut, New Jersey, the two Carolinas, and Georgia insisted on Protestantism. Two were content with the Christian religion; Delaware and Maryland. Four, Pennsylvania, Delaware, and the Carolinas, required assent to the divine inspiration of the Bible. Two, Pennsylvania and South Carolina, demanded a belief in heaven and hell. Three, New York, Maryland, and South Carolina, excluded ministers from civil office. Two, Pennsylvania and South Carolina, emphasized belief in one eternal God. One, Delaware, required assent to the doctrine of the Trinity. And five, New Hampshire, Massachusetts, Connecticut, Maryland, and South Carolina, adhered to a religious establishment."[15]

When the First Amendment was drafted "Something very like religious establishments, and a certain degree of compulsion in religious matters, still survived in the New England States."[16] Indeed, the

14 *Ibid.*, p. 20.
15 Cobb, Sanford H., *Rise of Religious Liberty in America* (1902), p. 507.
16 Crosskey, William Winslow, *Politics and the Constitution* (1953), II, 1060.

Constitution of Massachusetts at the time of the adoption of the First Amendment explicitly provided ". . . the people of this Commonwealth have a right to invest their legislature with power to authorize and require, and the legislature shall, from time to time, authorize and require the several towns, parishes, precincts, and other bodies-politic, or religious societies, to make suitable provision, at their own expense, for the institution for the public worship of God, and for the support and maintenance of public Protestant teachers of piety, religion, and morality, in all cases where such provision shall not be made voluntarily."

The adoption of the Federal Constitution in 1787 enunciated a different philosophy and the only one possible for a federated, pluralistic society. Moreover, as already noted, Article VI of the Constitution bans a "religious test" as a "qualification to any office or public trust under the United States." That goes back to "establishment" practices of the states before 1789. North Carolina once barred from office those who deny "the truth of the Protestant religion"; and South Carolina gave "equal religious and civil privileges" only to "denominations of protestants."[17] More than a century and a half later the banning of the test oath — a provision which bars a state, though its people are overwhelmingly Christian, from disquali-

[17] Cobb, *op. cit.*, pp. 504–505, n. 15.

fying even atheists for public positions (*Torcaso* v. *Watkins*, 367 U.S. 488) — put an end to state preferences for one religious group over another. The history of the First Amendment makes clear that all religions — not merely the numerous sects in the Christian faith — are included. As one delegate stated in the North Carolina debates on the Constitution, the abolition of a religious test would leave the Presidency open to members of any sect:

"For my part, in reviewing the qualifications necessary for a President, I did not suppose that the pope could occupy the President's chair. But let us remember that we form a government for millions not yet in existence. I have not the art of divination. In the course of four or five hundred years, I do not know how it will work. This is most certain, that Papists may occupy that chair, and Mahometans may take it. I see nothing against it."[18]

Benjamin Franklin, a singularly wise man, summed up the philosophy of separation of Church and State in a letter to Richard Price dated October 9, 1780 — prior to the adoption of the Bill of Rights. He said:

I am fully of your Opinion respecting religious Tests; but, tho' the People of Massachusetts have not in their new Constitution kept quite clear of them, yet, if we consider what that People were 100 years ago, we must allow they have gone great Lengths in Liberality of

[18] *Eliot's Debates* (1876), IV, 215.

Sentiment on religious Subjects; and we may hope for greater Degrees of Perfection, when their Constitution, some years hence, shall be revised. If Christian Preachers had continued to teach as Christ and his Apostles did, without Salaries, and as the Quakers now do, I imagine Tests would never have existed; for I think they were invented, not so much to secure Religion itself, as the Emoluments of it. When a Religion is good, I conceive that it will support itself; and, when it cannot support itself, and God does not take care to support it, so that its Professors are oblig'd to call for the help of the Civil Power, it is a sign, I apprehend, of its being a bad one. But I shall be out of my Depth, if I wade any deeper in Theology. . . .[19]

Early last century when the Public School Society dominated New York's school system, it introduced into the public schools books filled with literature that was anti–Roman Catholic. Those favoring a secular system must say with Hughes, the Catholic bishop who protested in 1840:

"We feel it unjust that such passages should be taught at all in the schools, to the support of which we are contributors as well as others."[20] What Hughes protested was a practice as invidious as the introduction into the public school system of books deriding Jews, downgrading Negroes, or ridiculing Puerto Ricans. That kind of policy, when it comes to religious

[19] Sparks, Jared, *Works of Franklin* (1944), pp. 505–506.
[20] O'Gorman, Thomas, *American Church History* (1915), p. 371.

matters, is hostile to the philosophy of the First Amendment.

The differences between the King James Version and the Catholic version of the Bible are indeed so great and the feelings concerning them so deep that in the 1840's the feeling generated became in part responsible for the Know-Nothing movement which cast an ugly shadow across the land.[21]

In the mid-nineteenth century, the Protestants were vocal in trying to keep the Bible in the schools, the Catholics being in dissent. It seems that the play is the same century after century, only the characters changing.

In 1842 complaints were numerous in New York and Pennsylvania that Catholic children were forced "to read the Protestant version of the Bible, and join in Protestant religious exercises." An effort to stop it was called the "Popish influence"; and Protestants were rallied to resist attempts "to kick the Bible from schools." There were riots and killings; and many houses were burned. A grand jury ascribed the trouble "to those who would exclude the Bible from the schools." The Catholics replied that the use of the King James Version of the Bible "led Catholic children to regard as authoritative a version rejected by the Church. In Baltimore the School Directors had provided Catholic children with the Catholic version.

[21] Beale, Howard Kennedy, *A History of Freedom of Teaching in American Schools* (1941), pp. 100–101.

Was it too much to expect the same measure of justice to Philadelphia?"[22]

New Jersey in 1953 took the correct constitutional view. When a New Jersey school board authorized the distribution of the Gideon Bible to students with their parents' permission, Jews and Catholics protested, claiming that the Gideon Bible is "a sectarian work of peculiar religious value and significance to members of the Protestant faith." The New Jersey Supreme Court held that the distribution of the Gideon Bible was state preference of one religion over another in violation of the state and federal constitutions (*Tudor* v. *Board of Education,* 14 N.J. 31). The Court said:

"To permit the distribution of the King James Version of the Bible in the public schools of this State would be to cast aside all the progress made in the United States and throughout New Jersey in the field of religious toleration and freedom. We would be renewing the ancient struggles among the various religious faiths to the detriment of all. This we must decline to do."

It was in that tradition that the Supreme Court of Wisconsin said that use of the King James Bible as a textbook in the public schools was "sectarian instruction" that violated the Wisconsin Constitution (*Weiss* v. *District Board,* 76 Wis. 177, 199) just as would

[22] McMaster, John B., *History of the People of the United States* (1910), VIII, 376, 381.

be the use of the Douay Version or the Book of Mormon or the Koran.

The 175th General Assembly of the United Presbyterian Church stated in May, 1963, "Bible reading and prayers as devotional acts tend toward indoctrination or meaningless ritual." Whenever a state prescribes a prayer for a public school, it indeed conducts a religious exercise, violating the neutrality required of the state by the First Amendment.

When it was proposed in 1860 that the British, then in command of India, introduce the Bible into public schools, Sir James Fitzjames Stephen wrote:

". . . if the experience and the controversies of the present generation have proved anything at all, they have shown that it is no part of the province of Governments to lay down the truth of any theological propositions whatever. . . .

"Why is the Government of India to take upon itself to assert to its subjects that the Song of Solomon and the Book of Esther are ultimate, absolute, and infallible truth, and that the Books of Wisdom, Ecclesiasticus, and the Maccabees are entitled to no authority at all?"[23]

---

[23] Stephen, Sir James Fitzjames, *Essays by a Barrister* (1862), pp. 154–156.

IV

The secular state is a different kind of state from what most of the people of the world have known. And its values are not always apparent to those who enter the mid-twentieth century from ghettoes where their very existence was in jeopardy.

". . . the status of the Jewish religion in Israel is not a simple one. One has to go back to the whole of Jewish history from the Bible to modern times to understand how religion often became a substitute for and even identical with Jewish national consciousness. Under the pressure of life in exile, love of land, history, language, culture and law were all poured into religious vessels. This is a problem which has not yet been completely solved, even now when a secular Jewish life is possible and this explains the extraordinary tolerance with which secular and non-religious Jews in Israel have yielded to the sentiments of the religious groups. This also explains the discomfort, even among non-religious Jews, over the fact that Jewish children in Israel are being educated in non-Jewish and even missionary schools."[1]

To those who are products of the free society of the Western world, the secular state is an advanced form of government, offering special rewards.

As already noted, our choice of the secular state was a philosophical choice as well as one founded on bitter experiences. The creation of the Board of Education in New York goes back to 1842, when the legislature, unable to divide public education funds among "quarreling and envious religious sects," created a public school system in which no "religious sectarian doctrine or tenet should be taught, inculcated, or practiced." [2] Had we not lived in communities where there was a multiplicity of sects, we might have followed a different path.

The secular state is advanced because it respects the conscience of every minority; it is advanced because it promotes religion more than it does sectarianism; it is advanced because it assures those who happen to make up the majority that the coercive power of government will not be used in their name to violate the conscience of any minority.

The secular state in India has emerged partly as a result of Western influence, but mostly on account of the Hindu philosophy.

[1] *New Outlook,* July–August 1963, pp. 7–8.
[2] Cubberley, Ellwood Patterson, *Public Education in the United States* (1918), p. 178.

"Gandhi's starting point was that of a religious man who, believing all religions to be true, accepted a theory of the state which fits in with the belief; hence the *secular* state. Nehru's starting point was that of a practical political thinker and leader who, while personally believing all religions to be mostly untrue, has provided for their freedom to function peacefully without prejudicing the democratic system; hence the *secular* state.

"Nehru defined the *secular* state as a state which protects all religions but does not favour one at the expense of others, and does not establish any religion as the official creed."[3]

India and the United States share to a large degree a philosophy respecting the relation of the State to the Church. Some two thousand years ago Jesus advised, "Render, therefore to Caesar the things that are Caesar's, and to God, the things that are God's." This political philosophy is the root of the present doctrine of separation of Church and State that obtains in the United States.

Separation of Church and State is also reflected in India's basic charter. Article 27 provides, "No person shall be compelled to pay any taxes, the proceeds of which are specifically appropriated in payment of expenses for the promotion or maintenance of any particular religion or religious denomination." Article

[3] *Indian and Foreign Review*, Nov. 1, 1963, p. 28.

28 (1) further provides: "No religious instruction shall be provided in any educational institution wholly maintained out of State funds." As Justice P. N. Sapru said in his Agra University lectures in 1953, "Our state has no established church. It assures to every citizen freedom to worship God in his own way and observes an attitude of strict neutrality towards all religions in this country."[4]

In 1814 when Norway adopted a constitution, it established the Evangelical-Lutheran faith as "the public religion of the State." Later, modifications were made enabling Roman Catholics to propagate their faith and establish parishes in Norway. But the words "Jesuits shall not be tolerated" remained in the Constitution. Finally, on November 1, 1956, they were stricken.[5]

Under an agreement that Franco made with the Vatican when he came to power in Spain, "The Church regained its place in the national budget. It insists on baptizing all children and has made the catechism obligatory in state schools."[6] "The Roman Catholic Church in Spain dominates education, is represented on all censorship boards for TV, radio, books and newspapers, and owns about 1,600 publications of various sorts. All schoolmasters, even in

[4] Douglas, William O., *We the Judges* (1958), p. 26.

[5] *U.N. Yearbook on Human Rights* (1956), p. 169.

[6] Bates, Miner Searle, *Religious Liberty: An Inquiry* (1945), p. 18.

state schools, are supposed to be practicing Catholics."[7]

Efforts to give Protestants a greater degree of religious liberty have been powerfully opposed. In 1964 the Archbishop of Sion and Catholic Vicar-General for Spain's armed forces protested those attempts. Full religious liberty, he maintained, would produce "the enslavement of the conscience of Catholic peoples." The proposed religious liberty measure, which the Archbishop opposed, would enable Protestants to operate schools and newspapers; but it would keep a ban on missionary activities of Protestants. Moreover, under Spanish law every new measure that changes the status of Protestants in Spain must be approved by the Vatican. These restrictions on Protestants are recognized in the agreements establishing United States Air Force bases in Spain. Under those agreements an American Protestant chaplain may not contact Spanish Protestants.

The Church of England is in many ways an "established" church today. Bishops have seats in Parliament as Lords of Parliament and as a *quid pro quo* the Crown has a voice in their appointment.[8]

This English practice had vast repercussions on these shores in the eighteenth century. John Adams wrote:

[7] Thomas, Hugh, "The Balance of Forces in Spain," *Foreign Affairs,* 41 (1962), 208, 210.

[8] *Spectator,* July 31, 1964, p. 147.

"If any gentleman supposes this controversy to be nothing to the present purpose, he is grossly mistaken. It spread an universal alarm against the authority of Parliament. It excited a general and just apprehension, that bishops, and dioceses, and churches, and priests, and tithes, were to be imposed on us by Parliament. It was known that neither king, nor ministry, nor archbishops, could appoint bishops in America, without an act of Parliament; and if Parliament could tax us, they could establish the Church of England, with all its creeds, articles, tests, ceremonies, and tithes, and prohibit all other churches, as conventicles and schism shops." [9]

Islam evolved differently. Its religion, often associated with reactionary if not chauvinistic forces, became the vehicle of Arab consciousness and from the Arabs was passed on to peoples of many races. A scholar has recently asked about this Islamic history, "How can religious values, backed by a tradition of hundreds of years, be reconciled with modern social and political life?" [10] As Iqbal, the great poet from Lahore, has put it: "The task facing the Moslem of today is stupendous. He has to think out the whole system of Islam afresh, without severing its links with the past." [11]

[9] Adams, John, *Life and Work of John Adams* (1856), X, 288.

[10] *New Outlook*, July–August 1963, p. 19.

[11] *Ibid.*, p. 21.

[39]

In the world of Islam laws are drawn in accord with Koranic principles; Church and State are subtly blended; the line between secular and sectarian authority is confused. Turkey, for some five hundred years ending with World War I, was indeed governed by a council of *mullahs* (priests), who found the general welfare within the Koran. That book, while rich in moral precepts, contains nothing concerning penicillin, mathematics, the atom, or electric energy. So it was that Turkey, peering intently into the Koran, missed the entire Industrial Revolution. And it took Ataturk to bring her to her senses. What Ataturk did belittled the Koran no more than the California Institute of Technology by its researches belittles the Bible. The eclipse of Turkey under sectarian control brings a shattering realization that the end product of sectarian political control can be stagnation.

Old influences are hard to change. While Ataturk kept Turkey on the narrow *secular* path, agitation for a resumption of sectarian control picked up on his death. One result is that today in Turkey religious education has been reinstated in Turkish public schools.[12]

In sectarian circles hunger for secular power is still strong the world over.

Implicit in most religions is a tenet of the superiority or supremacy of the particular faith and a branding of all other creeds as "false." Religious

[12] *Ibid.*, p. 21.

[40]

groups have waged war against the "infidels" or "heathens." Such indeed was the battlecry of Pope Urban II, who launched the Crusades and pitted Christian against Moslem in a bloody and senseless struggle. Religious communities discriminate against other religious groups in the same community, a recent episode of the kind to reach the level of world news being the action of Vietnam's Roman Catholic government against the Buddhists and its subsequent overthrow by predominantly Buddhist troops — a coup sparked in part by bitter religious rivalry. In countless minor ways, religious communities the world over practice discrimination against rival religious groups in their neighborhoods.

No religious group has activated the principle more than the Moslems. Libertarian Moslems who frequent international circles protest against the practice as vigorously as libertarian Protestants protested the anti-Catholic attitude that carried Alfred E. Smith to defeat in the presidential campaign of 1928.

The world over the idea seems the same — that one's own religious group should be on top. We of the West are less explicit about it than the Moslems have been. But throughout the years we and the Moslems have walked the same path.

The Koran is in many ways franker, for it admonishes the faithful to "fight for the religion of God against those who fight against you," "kill them wherever you find them," "for temptation to idolatry is more grievous than slaughter." A militant aspect of the Islamic faith became front-page news in 1964. A strand of hair of the prophet Mohammed was stolen from a mosque in Kashmir where it had been kept for three hundred years. Thousands of Moslems took to the streets and many died in demonstrations which continued until the sacred hair was recovered. This episode proved to some Moslems that even their religion and culture are not safe in India.

Boycott of members of other churches has been common in all lands. Here again the Moslems have been more open. The Koran encourages the boycott of the "idolaters" by cutting off trade and communication. All "people of the book" — those "unto whom the scriptures have been delivered" (which include at least Christians and Jews and in practice others such as Zoroastrians) — are to "be reduced low" and required to "pay tribute by right of subjection." This meant that affluent members of a religious minority could buy their religious freedom from Moslem governments. The affluent people did just that, paying whatever price was negotiated; and that explains the survival of our vestigial Zoroastrians, who in time moved to India and are now known in Bombay as the Parsees. That explains the survival to this day of Jews in Afghanistan. But the poor could not pay tribute; and so to survive they succumbed and became Moslems.

Even today, April 24 is "Martyr Day" for members

of the Armenian Church throughout the world. This is the date of the Turkish Massacre of 1915, when the Turkish government attempted to force the Armenians to accept Islamic doctrine. As Congressman Sisk of California recently said in testimony before the House Judiciary Committee on the Becker Amendment: [13]

"We see here the direct and terrible climax of state-sponsored and established religion. We see a religion possessing the police and military power of a nation used to suppress and wipe out another religion. We see the awful power of religious emotion, armed with political power to slaughter all those who were to them non-believers."

"The representative Muslim believes that only Islam can regenerate the world, and that sooner or later his religion will dominate all nations." [14] Those who see Africa in transition will see some of this enthusiasm in action. For as we started the 1960's, Islam had about 87 million African converts, as compared with 22 million for Christianity.

When it comes to obtaining an "established" religion, the Moslem is not in the minority. But he is as reluctant as any to give up any authority that is once acquired; and he is as eager as any other to have his church "established" (in whole or in part) as

[13] Hearings, House Judiciary Committee 88th Cong., 2d Sess. Pt. I, Serial 4, p. 535.

[14] Freund, C. J., "Muslim Education in West Pakistan," *Religious Education,* 56 (1961), 31.

the official religion. "For the Arab, religion is the value that comes first in politics, in social point of view, and in any program of fundamental reform," as one authority describes this religious frame of reference.[15] From a Moslem's point of view, education is a religious activity like prayer, fasting, and preaching. In the public schools in Pakistan, for example, students are required to study the Koran up to the eighth class and in some areas in high schools as well. The Koran is memorized in Arabic and the opening verses are recited in Arabic each morning when schools convene.

"The Koran is thought to be the most widely read book in the world, because the Moslems, even though they are only half as numerous as the Christians in the world, use it not only as their Bible but also as the textbook from which virtually every Moslem who can read Arabic has learned to do so." [16]

The introduction of a chant from the Koran into a school is the "establishment" of a part of the Islamic religion, just as the requirement of circumcision would be the "establishment" of another part. For a state of our Union to require either would flout the Establishment Clause of the First Amendment, which is as applicable to the States (by reason of the Fourteenth Amendment) as it is to the federal government. That

[15] Rugh, "Arab Countries of the Near East," in *Comparative Education* (Moehlman & Roucek, eds.) (1952), p. 453.
[16] *Ibid.*, p. 454.

[44]

is the teaching of *Abington School District* v. *Schempp* (374 U.S. 203). Yet we have in America religious groups as avid as any Moslem community to put their religious faith up front by getting state support.

The Islamic religion is spreading fast — at a pace four times that of Christianity in Africa. It spreads here, too — there were twenty-six mosques in the nation in 1964, Washington, D.C., having a mosque, and many areas having Islamic communities. Moslems occupy governmental posts, at least one having sat in Congress. In time Moslems will control some of our school boards. In time devout Moslems may want their prayer in our schools; and if Protestant sects can get their prayers past the barriers of the First Amendment, the same passage would be guaranteed for Moslems, as Islam is one of the great religions of the world. The Moslem prayer that would open our schools is composed of the first passages of the Koran, which is, according to George Sale's edition of 1853, "held in great veneration by the Mohammedans, who give it several other honourable titles; as the chapter of *prayer*, of *praise*, of *thanksgiving*, of *treasure*, etc. They esteem it as the quintessence of the whole Koran, and often repeat it in their devotions both public and private, as the Christians do the Lord's Prayer." This is the passage which youngsters in Moslem nations recite in Arabic at the opening of every school day:

"In the name of the most merciful God. Praise be

to God, the Lord of all creatures; the most merciful, the king of the day of judgment. Thee do we worship, and of thee do we beg assistance. Direct us in the right way, in the way of those to whom thou hast been gracious; not of those who go astray."

This prayer is pregnant with meaning. Sale's edition gives the following explanation of it:

"This last sentence contains a petition, that God would lead the supplicants into the true religion, by which is meant the Mohammedan, in the Koran often called *the right way*; in this place more particularly defined to be, *the way of those to whom God hath been gracious,* that is, of the prophets and faithful who preceded Mohammed; under which appellations are also comprehended the Jews and Christians, such as they were in the times of their primitive purity, before they had deviated from their respective institutions; *not the way of the modern* Jews, whose signal calamities are marks of the just *anger* of God against them for their obstinacy and disobedience; *nor of the* Christians *of this age*, who have departed from the true doctrine of Jesus, and are bewildered in a labyrinth of error."

Our most popular religious sects do not lack a like degree of partisanship.

V

E<small>VERY</small> student of the subject ultimately faces the disorder which the mixture of sectarian and secular authority generates — either disorder between the majority sect and minority ones, or disorder between the church and the government, sometimes leading to the latter's overthrow by the former.[1] It is discord between the sects with which we Americans have been most frequently concerned.

George Washington, though at one time supporting the proposition that all churches should have equal claim to tax revenues, later stated in a letter to George Mason dated October 3, 1785, that it would be better that the matter be dropped, for "it will rankle and perhaps convulse, the State."[2] Once public school prayers are the prize, a bitter contest is on for control of the school board. Only those who have gone through that political experience know the full depth and power of religious animosities.

[1] Thomas, Hugh, "The Balance of Forces in Spain," *Foreign Affairs*, 41 (1962), 208, 211–213.
[2] *Writings of Washington* (Fitzpatrick ed.), XXVIII, 285.

School boards have been torn asunder by contests over whose prayer will be said in the public schools, whose catechism will be read. Religious contests over secular power have been among the bloodiest in history; and though free of blood, they have no equal in emotional content unless it be a racial argument.

Our experiences in the nineteenth century showed how divisive sectarian education in public schools can become. The teachings of the New Testament — even the story of the Good Samaritan — are anathema to some Jews. A rabbi testified in the *Schempp* case (374 U.S. 203):

You have the story of this very sick person lying on the road. There are three people who pass by, a priest, a Levite, and a Samaritan. . . . [The] three divisions were priests, descendants of Aaron who were priests officiating in the temple who had to be pure in order to enter the temple — "pure," I mean ritually pure — the Levites, whose purity was not expected to be so great but they were also descendants of Aaron, and Israelites, ordinary Israelites, who were not subject to the laws of purity quite as much.

Now, think of the story as it must have been told in those days. A priest passes by. He sees what he thinks is a dead body. The laws of purity apply to him. He wouldn't touch it because he would make himself impure and couldn't officiate in the temple. He passes it by. It is a cruel act. He should have forgotten the laws of impurity and should have attended to the burial of the person, but he preferred — being a stickler for the law he preferred to take care of his purity.

Then comes the Levite; the same thing.

Then, along comes an Israelite to whom the laws of impurity do not apply in the same thing and he attends to the person who is lying on the ground.

That story told in this way, as it must have been, has a moral effect and a good story. It is a good story. What happened? In the story as it came to be told the Israelite was obviously removed and the Samaritan put in. Why a Samaritan? Well, the Samaritans and Israelites in those days were not on good terms. Very likely the Samaritan was deliberately put in as a slap at the Jews of that day who refused to join the Christian Church, because the story on the face of it must have been, must have included priest, Levite, Israelite. That was the division. There was no such division as priest, Levite, Samaritan.

Now, you tell this story in a school to a Jewish child or in the presence of a Jewish child and a Christian child and the Christian child has every right to say, "See, you come of a people that is cruel, and that doesn't understand the decencies of life." And even if the Jewish child is not told that, it is made to feel that, and I submit to you, sir, that that destroys all the moral value of the story. And I don't think that that kind of story ought to be read in a public school where there are — in any public school — because it makes for division rather than for union.

The First Amendment and the ban on the test oath were designed to keep religion from being a divisive force. Tolerance of all religions, preference for none, were the means whereby harmony was to be created out of diversity, where a "multiplicity of sects" was to create community and national unity.

Doctrine and creed have always contained seeds of disunion. Fasting on Saturdays and the consecration of unleavened bread were the occasion — though perhaps not the basic cause — of the schism between West and East in A.D. 1054.[3] As Paul Blanshard says, ". . . in a society which is as pluralistic as ours there is virtually no religious or ceremonial phenomenon that is not sectarian to somebody." [4]

The broader the support for a nondenominational prayer, the greater the likelihood that the groups at either extreme will be offended. The very religious will find it at best meaningless; at worst, contrary to their own beliefs. Rabbi Edward E. Klein testified at the hearings before the House Judiciary Committee on the Becker Amendment: [5]

"I think one can find Jewish theological principles in the Lord's Prayer but the mere title of the Lord's Prayer as the Lord's Prayer indicating the Lord as Jesus would make it unacceptable for Jews. There is no prayer, really, in the Jewish literature that occupies the role that the Lord's Prayer does in Christianity.

"It is a beautiful prayer. It can be traced to Jewish

[3] See Fortescue, Adrian, *Orthodox Eastern Church* (1916), p. 178; Tozer, Henry F., *The Church and the Eastern Empire* (1900), ch. 9.
[4] Blanshard, Paul, *Religion and the Schools: The Great Controversy* (1963), p. 89.
[5] Hearings, House Committee on Judiciary, 88th Cong., 2nd Sess., Serial 9, Part III, p. 1999.

[50]

sources but it has become the central prayer of Christianity and would not be acceptable because it has become the prayer of the Lord Jesus Christ."

The sum of this experience does not mean that religious rituals or sectarian instruction may be allowed if a particular community happens to be so homogeneous on religious matters as to arouse no opposition. For one sect to fasten itself on the school system when the political climate is right foreshadows trouble when the complexion of a community changes.

Yet as Edmund Cahn stated, "the American principle of separation of church and state has never rested on exclusively secular grounds." The danger was not only in a secular state but to "religion itself." Cahn said, ". . . considering the overwhelming power and resources of the modern state, the church and religion need the protecting shield of separation today much more than the state itself."

Cahn goes on to point out an advantage in the secular state that is commonly overlooked. It is a protection accorded the majority as well as the minority. The First Amendment "makes it ethically safe to belong to the majority. By separating church and state, it assures the rarest, and perhaps the most excellent, of all civil rights: the constitutional right not to persecute." [6]

Separation of Church and State is necessary for a

[6] Cahn, Edmund, "On Government and Prayer," *N. Y. U. L. Rev.* 37 (1962), 381, 983, 984, 985.

pluralistic society. Then the state is unable to judge in religious matters and the church is incapable of judging in political matters.[7] All sectarian groups flourish because none sits in authority over the others. If religious and political considerations come into conflict, the political agencies resolve them. For the political agencies — not a church group — represent all the constituents in society. The Reverend Edward L. Peet, a Methodist, of Haywood, California, reminded us of the consequences of the alternative course: [8]

In the historical separation of church and state as interpreted by the Supreme Court the churches of America have prospered as nowhere in the world.

Go to Latin America and to Spain where the churches have compelled the state to take sides in religion and to propagate religion in every way and there you see the churches in full retreat and Christianity a byword for reaction and tyranny. Go to Scandinavia where there have been state churches for generations and religion in the schools and there the churches are empty. . . .

The public school is a tax-supported institution and no religious exercise can be devised to satisfy or to please the many kinds of American taxpayers. Some of these are Christians — Catholics and Protestants, some are Jews, some are Buddhists, and some are from the 35 per cent of Americans who make no religious profession at all. I say, keep religion out of the schools and put it

[7] Beth, Loren P., *The American Theory of Church and State* (1958), pp. 153–154.

[8] Hearings, *supra* note 5, pp. 2001–2002.

into the homes and encourage the churches to promote it everywhere.

. . . the school as the instrument of the state is and must be religiously neutral. No other way is decent or practical in pluralistic America. . . .

All compulsory religion, and this would be compulsory on all children, is a denial of the spirit of Christian love. Here in the classroom, for example, are children from non-Christian homes or from homes where there is a sincere opposition to religion. Is it right to force them into our mold? Is it right to expose them to the ridicule of other children because they don't go along? And any of it could do harm to the very Christian cause we so zealously support.

VI

THE Court has never squarely decided the constitutionality of state or federal aid to religious schools, though, as already noted, a broad *dictum* in *Everson* v. *Board of Education* (330 U.S. 1, 16) precludes it.

The Act of December 16, 1963 (77 Stat. 363) authorizes federal grants to institutions of higher education, including parochial schools, for construction of "structures, or portions thereof, especially designed for instruction or research in the natural or physical sciences, mathematics, modern foreign languages, or engineering, or for use as a library." Federal loans may be made to parochial schools, as well as to other institutions of higher education "for the construction of academic facilities," including a facility used "for sectarian instruction or as a place for religious worship" or as part of a "school or department of divinity."

When does a private institution such as a school or hospital become a state or federal agency?

Individuals, churches, private schools, homeowners

can be as selective as they want in their associations. They can shun one race, one church group, one nationality as they choose — and cater only to those they like. Business has broader responsibilities under modern law; but private groups normally may practice such discrimination as they choose. Government agencies, however, speak for the state or federal government; and they may not transgress any of the civil rights guaranteed by the Constitution and Bill of Rights since those guarantees are prohibitions against governmental action. If a private school or private hospital receives governmental financial aid does it become a governmental agency? Suppose government finances a private group that practices segregation of the races. Suppose it finances the teaching of a particular religious faith. Suppose the private group that it finances allows racial or religious discrimination in its employment practices. Are those practices allowable in light of the association of government with the project? The question has been stirred in the courts (see *Simkins* v. *Moses H. Cone Memorial Hospital,* 323 F. 2d, 959).

If the "private" institution has become "public" by reason of financial aid or control, then it cannot refuse to serve people because of race (*Burton* v. *Wilmington Parking Authority,* 365 U.S. 715). If it is such, then it cannot discriminate against customers or patients on the grounds of creed or belief. If a church hospital has become a state agency by reason

[55]

of the kind and manner of state aid it has received, then it cannot any more than the state itself discharge personnel because they believe in birth control, because they belong to a minority religious group, or because of their ideology or their nationality. These are some of the large — and as yet unsettled — constitutional questions centering on state and federal aid to parochial and other private institutions. Questions of like dimensions are involved in our overseas activities.

Some of our military funds have been used overseas to help a religious school with its building program.

The Alliance for Progress has made grants to religious institutions to carry on designated educational projects.

One religious group was designated as the exclusive outlet in one country for Food for Peace, though other religious groups also operate there.

Part of the problem of Food for Peace is seen in caricature in Peter Sellers's movie *Heavens Above*. In that comedy, one minister got free food from a wealthy parishioner which he then dispensed under the auspices of the church. Other churches lost their members, who flocked to the church that had free food. Is that likely to happen when we give one overseas religious group a monopoly in the distribution of our Food for Peace? What competitive advantage over other religions does that particular church have if it receives that monopoly power? Does that amount to a *pro tanto* "establishment" in the meaning of the First Amendment?

The problems posed by Madison and Jefferson appear in different settings today, but they are in main the same. At home and abroad we must face them as long as we live under a Constitution that guarantees diversity for all men. From the very beginning, our multireligious community has had many debates, some of them acrimonious. They have largely concerned matters on the domestic scene. In the months and years ahead they will increasingly implicate foreign affairs. For there are at all times many who would openly or covertly merge Church and State; and they act with the greatest patriotism abroad, the better to combat Communism, they think. Future policies concerning Church and State at home and abroad make it imperative that we all become immersed in the history of the Establishment Clause of the First Amendment.

There is enough mucilage to hold our society together without the regimentation of any particular theological doctrine. What Stephen said of England a century ago is true of America today:

"After a controversy which began with Catholic Emancipation and the repeal of the Test and Corporation Acts, and which displayed its last relics of vitality in the debates on the admission of Jews to Parliament, it has been practically decided that there is a very large province of human affairs, involving moral

[57]

responsibilities of the highest possible importance, in which people can co-operate with the greatest mutual advantage without any common profession whatever of theological belief, and in spite of theological differences of the most extreme kind." [9]

Christianity has sufficient inner strength to survive and flourish on its own.[10] It does not need state subsidies, nor state privileges, nor state prestige. The more it obtains state support the greater it curtails human freedom. For what the Roman Catholics, the Baptists, or the Presbyterians can command of the public treasury or in other public support, so in time can the Moslems or the Mormons as they grow politically stronger. The nonconformist — he who belongs to a dissenting sect or who worships in a more esoteric way or whose relation to the universe has only philosophical moorings — pays the price when public institutions which he supports promote sectarian purposes.

As to prayers in public schools, we should remember that public schools are supported by all sects — nonbelievers as well as believers, by minorities as well as by the majority. In America public schools have a unique public function to perform. They are designed to train American students in an atmosphere that is free from parochial, sectarian, and separatist influences. The heritage they seek to instill is one

9 Stephen, *Essays by a Barrister* (1862), p. 154.
10 *Commonweal,* September 6, 1963, p. 530.

that all sects, all races, all groups have in common. It is not atheistic nor is it theistic. It is a civic and patriotic heritage that transcends all differences among people, that bridges the gaps in sectarian creeds, that cements all in a common unity of nationality, and that reduces differences that emphasis on race, creed, and sect only accentuate.

Appendix

THE proposed Becker Amendment offered by Congressman Frank J. Becker of the State of New York:

Sec. 1.   Nothing in this Constitution shall be deemed to prohibit the offering, reading from or listening to prayers or biblical scriptures, if participation therein is on a voluntary basis, in any governmental or public school, institution, or place.

Sec. 2.   Nothing in this Constitution shall be deemed to prohibit making reference to belief in, reliance upon, or invoking the aid of God or a Supreme Being in any governmental or public document, proceeding, activity, ceremony, school, institution or place, or upon any coinage, currency, or obligation of the United States.

Sec. 3.   Nothing in this article shall constitute an establishment of religion.

The Hearings on this proposed Amendment and others were before the Committee on the Judiciary, House of Representatives, Eighty-eighth Congress, Second session, April, May, and June 3, 1964, Serial No. 9, Parts 1–3. And see Preliminary Staff Study, Committee Print on Proposed Amendments to the Constitution Relating to

School Prayers, Bible Reading, etc., A Staff Study for the House Judiciary Committee, March 24, 1964.

Antieau, Chester J. et al., *Freedom From Federal Establishment*, 1964, 272 pp.

This is our most recent historical work dealing with the Establishment Clause. It is a painstaking work that treats in a discriminating way with the English, colonial, and pre-First Amendment materials. It is the initial publication of the Institute for Church-State Law of the Georgetown University Law Center, and is pre-eminent for its scholarship.

Blanshard, Paul. *Religion and the Schools.* 1963. 265 pp.

This volume is an ardent brief in support of the decisions in the *Prayer Cases,* the opinions being printed in appendices. One of the most stimulating and provocative parts of the book concerns the opposition of the Roman Catholic hierarchy to President Kennedy on federal aid to religious schools and the resulting federal legislation. The book puts many of these controversial issues into sharper focus by telling us of their counterparts in other parts of the world.

Costanzo, Joseph F. *This Nation Under God.* 1964. 448 pp.

This is a sturdy Jesuit critique of the First Amendment and the Court decisions under it. While it is critical of some judicial rulings, it is careful to put them in fair perspective. He urges more leeway for legislatures in this field than courts have generally allowed. Though a protagonist, he writes with restraint and with tolerance for opposed views.

[61]

Drinan, Robert F., *Religion, the Courts, and Public Policy.* 1963. 261 pp.

This work is an analysis by a thoughtful Jesuit of court decisions under the Free Exercise and Establishment Clauses. While he writes from the Roman Catholic point of view, his message of toleration is addressed to Catholics as well as to those Protestants who still believe that public schools are really liberal Protestant schools teaching a nonsectarian Christianity.

Religion and the Public Order. Edited by Donald A. Giannella, 1964, 338 pp.

This book contains articles and comments of over a dozen men, gathered from the proceedings of the Institute of Church and State at Villanova University for 1963. These papers touch mostly on American experience; but some references to foreign practices abroad are also present. A variety of viewpoints is represented; and a concluding part comments on them.

This volume touches not only the central items in the conflict that rages but sensibly goes afield to explore the educational aspects of the problem. Is it the function of public education to teach morality? Does state or federal aid to parochial schools violate the First Amendment (a) where it has not strings attached or (b) where it is allocated to a specific end such as nuclear physics?

Greene, Evarts B., *The Revolutionary Generation, 1763–1790.* Edited by Schlesinger and Fox, Macmillan, 1943. 485 pp.

This is a lucid presentation of the environment out of which the First Amendment emerged, especially Chapter V dealing with Church-State problems prior to our Revolution.

Huegli, Albert George. *Church and State Under God.* 1964. 512 pp.

This book is a collection of essays written by Lutheran authorities in various disciplines. It is a robust and refreshing treatment, comparing throughout Calvinist, Puritan, Anglican, and Roman Catholic positions on Church and State with the classic Lutheran tradition. Some overseas experiences and observations are included; and a close examination of Lutheran thought shows that it too lacks unanimity. A searching examination of education and the relationship of Church and State to it both historically and philosophically, is made. The case *pro* and *con* as respects parochial schools is stated and many peripheral subjects such as free textbooks and school lunches are covered. This is a very useful reference book with comprehensive footnotes and a good index.

Johnson, Alvin Walter, and Yost, Frank H. *Separation of Church and State in the United States.* 1948. 279 pp.

This book covers much more than is conventionally included in treatments of the Free Exercise and Establishment Clauses of the First Amendment. It is a penetrating work that challenges many preconceptions. It is highly factual in content and therefore most valuable as a reference.

Marnell, William Henry. *The First Amendment.* 1964. 247 pp.

This is a valuable review of the background and history of Church and State in America with primary emphasis upon origins and early practices. The author is less concerned with working out with logic alone the contentious issues that beset us; rather he searches for a strongly pragmatic bias in the American temperament for an accommodation between two regimes that must live harmoniously together if the Free Society is to survive.

McGrath, John J., *Church and State in American Law*. 1962. 414 pp.

This is a collection of cases and other materials bearing on various aspects of the separation of Church and State. It includes state and federal decisions, dealing with attempted control by state governments of ecclesiastical affairs as well as with state aid to religious schools, free exercise of religion, and the Establishment Clause. It also prints historical documents from our colonial period bearing on these questions.

This is a valuable reference book, especially for those who do not have ready access to law libraries.

The Wall Between Church and State. Edited by Dollin H. Oaks, 1963. 179 pp.

This is a product of a Conference on Church and State held at the University of Chicago. It consists of an introduction and of eight papers on various aspects of the problem. Some are *pro*, some are *con* the Supreme Court decisions on prayer in public schools and on other religious matters. All are provocative and an aid to rational and unemotional discussion.

Pfeffer, Leo. *Church and State in the United States*. 1964. 660 pp.

This is a one-volume edition with roots primarily in Anson Phelps Stokes's *Church and State* first published in 1950. This is by scholastic standards the most comprehensive, painstaking volume in the field that covers all aspects of state meddling in church affairs as well as the many ramifications of the Free Exercise and Establishment Clauses. The book covers not only court decisions but American history bearing on these religious issues, including the Know-Nothing movement and the American Party. It is less a plea for one point of view than an array of relevant data for the thoughtful reader. It is indeed our best single reference book.

Regan, Richard J., *American Pluralism and the Catholic Conscience*. 1962. 288 pp.

This is an even-handed Roman Catholic version of the issues involved in the Free Exercise and Establishment Clauses written by a distinguished Jesuit. The Catholic position is not monolithic; there are separatist arguments in that community as well as in the others. This gives a fair and challenging account of the American Catholic viewpoint.

Rice, Charles E., *The Supreme Court and Public Prayer*. 1964. 202 pp.

This is a resolute, thoughtful dissent from the Court's *prayer cases* with an attempt to anticipate their impact on collateral issues, e.g. state aid to parochial schools. It reviews at the end the means of avoiding the results of those decisions — legislative limitation of the Court's appellate jurisdiction and constitutional amendments.

Wright, Louis Booker, *The Cultural Life of the American Colonies, 1607–1763*. 1957. 292 pp.

This book, like that of Greene mentioned above, is an illuminating account of the environment out of which the First Amendment emerges. That is not its only target; yet its Chapter Four — "Diversity of Religions" — is one of our best historical accounts.

[65]